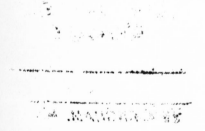

J. B. Priestley

by IVOR BROWN

Published for The British Council
and the National Book League
by Longmans, Green & Co.

Two shillings and sixpence net

Mr. J. B. Priestley, critic, essayist, story-teller, broadcaster, novelist and playwright, has the rare distinction, for an English writer, of being well known all over the world. He has the power to entertain in an exceptional degree, and his plays in particular are the work of a man who provokes thought.

He was born in Bradford, Yorkshire, in 1894, and ever since his first appearance as an author in 1919, he has poured out a succession of books of very diverse kinds. At first it was as an essayist that he won recognition, a recent example of his skill in this field being his *William Hazlitt* in the present series. Then, gradually changing over to fiction, he achieved resounding success in 1929 with his long, episodic and robust novel *The Good Companions*. From 1932 onwards he became more and more engaged in the drama, experimenting ceaselessly and with unflagging vigour.

Mr. Ivor Brown, from his long and intimate knowledge of the stage, is particularly suited to write an appreciation of Priestley the man of the theatre. His study includes other aspects of Mr. Priestley's achievements, but it is for his assessment of his plays that it has especial value.

In 1951, Mr. Brown edited *The Priestley Companion*, which included many-sided riches chosen from Mr. Priestley's work. Mr. Brown is himself an author of originality and distinction, and was from 1942 to 1948 editor of the *Observer*.

Bibliographical Series
of Supplements to 'British Book News'
on Writers and Their Work

*

GENERAL EDITOR
Geoffrey Bullough

J. B. PRIESTLEY

J. B. PRIESTLEY

by

Joan Carnegie

IVOR BROWN

PUBLISHED FOR
THE BRITISH COUNCIL
AND THE NATIONAL BOOK LEAGUE
BY LONGMANS, GREEN & CO.

LONGMANS, GREEN AND CO. LTD
48 Grosvenor Street, London, W.1

*Associated companies, branches and
representatives throughout the world*

First published 1957
Revised edition 1964
First and revised editions © Ivor Brown 1957, 1964

*Printed in Great Britain by
F. Mildner & Sons, London, E.C.1*

J. B. PRIESTLEY

I

OF THE English writers who were most active and eminent in the second quarter of the twentieth century and who are no less busy and conspicuous in the third, J. B. Priestley has been the most fertile and the most versatile. A glance at his bibliography will show the range and quantity of his output: he has been, amid all his writing of essays, criticism, novels and plays, a prolific journalist with a wide variety of topics and a first-class broadcaster reviewing the social landscape of the years. He delights in controversy and finds time for travel, being a frequent visitor to the American continent. He is also a meta-physician and holds strong views about the nature of Time which, for him, transcends our ordinary notions of the clock. He has always been ready to face a new challenge or oppor-tunity; he has directed and acted in his own plays and he has written a special series of Television features, which meant the mastering of yet another technique. Nobody could be more radically different from the escapist type of *petit maître* —a title which Sir Max Beerbohm delighted to earn—and from the deliberate, secluded, fastidious man of letters such as E. M. Forster, than the fiercely energetic and rapidly productive Priestley.

It is easy to say of his less important work that he would have written better if he had written less and if he had given his typewriters (he is no penman) a more frequent holiday. But such a judgement would be grossly unjust if it were not accompanied by the acknowledgement that he has added high quality of conception, perception, and description to the great quantity of his creations and his commentaries. Time and again he has shown that in the swift etching of a character, either in a novel or for the stage, he has a most vivid appreciation of the human comedy and a command of wit and of sympathy, qualities rare in combination, that puts him among the highest rank of verbal portrait-painters. Furthermore, his reporting of a journey and of the economic, as well as the physical, panorama of the places visited, has revealed a brilliant power of observation and description.

A man of so many parts and such prodigal authorship is to be judged by his best: he can well afford to be uneven who has such heights among the lesser countryside of his work, and the top of Priestley's achievement has been of impressive strength, while his ability to add a genial humour to the muscularity of his world-survey has given his work a constant warmth of humanity.

In an age of much cloudy writing he has never failed to be clear. If he has written, as such a man must, plenty that is controversial and rouses the desire to contradict, he has never written a book, a play, or an article that is vague. One always knows where one is with Priestley: it may be ground that one cannot share, but it is ground that is excellently mapped. He has written for the general reader and not for the intellectual specialist. Although, especially in his latest work, he has developed doubts about the value of pure reason and a taste for what some would call the super-rational and others would dismiss as the whimsical, he has always stated his case for the unusual in the idiom and vocabulary of use and wont. If he turns to mysticism, he does not mystify, and the fact that his thinking is restless has never inclined him to be obscure. He deals in theories without being the abstract or the baffling theorist: Walt Whitman was accused of contradicting himself; he retorted that of course he contradicted himself. 'I am large. I contain multitudes.' Priestley could say the same: he has never failed to show himself a large, a multitudinous man.

John Boynton Priestley's experience of life began in Bradford where he was born in 1894. He has vividly described his father in a book of reflections amid travel called *Midnight on the Desert*. Priestley Senior was a schoolmaster, 'not a born scholar but a born teacher, with an almost ludicrous passion for acquiring and imparting knowledge'. He was a public-spirited citizen, not a dull ministrant of good works and good causes, but brisk and humorous in his service of committees and the public welfare. The home life was naturally simple, but a little money could be made to go a long way. So the frugality was mixed with the hospitality of 'open house' and high spirits. Round about was the Yorkshire mixture of hard work and a hard, happy search for enjoyment.

There were also Radical or Socialist politics to formulate the indignation of the young at the mess and muddle of their industrial inheritance. There was rich character in his friends and neighbours, and there is a fine tribute to the vitality of that company and to its home-made humour, songs, and music—nothing was laid on then by the radio's horn of plenty—in one of his novels, *Bright Day*. A keen-witted youngster in the Bradford of fifty years ago could have much value if he took his chances. Priestley has some-times featured himself playfully in his essays as a notable practitioner of Grumbling. But he has never followed the habit so dear to many authors of whining about his child-hood. His memories of domesticity are cordial. The office-work in the wool trade to which he went, after schooling in Bradford, meant long hours and a dull routine, but the young man knew how to cope with boredom: there were his fellow-workers to watch and the offerings of town and country to relish, a gallery seat at the Theatre Royal, a week-end in the Yorkshire dales and on the great wilderness of the fells, and then, perhaps, with a few of the golden sovereigns which bought so much, a voyage on a cargo boat from Hull to Denmark and the savouring of a bright new scene.

Into this broke the war of 1914, and Priestley, an early volunteer, had long, combatant years in the local regiment, the Duke of Wellington's, and later in the Devons. Of his war memories he did not write until later, but he described with great feeling in his book called *English Journey* a gathering of his fellow servicemen with the terrible gaps in their ranks. On demobilization he went, with a Government

grant, to Trinity Hall at Cambridge, where he read English
Literature, and where he might have stayed on in academic
life. But Cambridge, with all its personal freedoms and its
beauty of scene, seems to have made small appeal. He has not
brought it into his books and he was eager to leave it for
London. He would not teach others to be bookmen: he
would write books himself. So he took the adventure and
soon was engaged as a busy critic in the weekly reviews, and
as a reader to the publishing firm of John Lane, in which
house there had long been shrewd attention paid to the
arrival of new talent.

II

'I flit from one kind of work to another, partly sustained
by a very genuine interest in the technical problem of all
forms of writing. I have always wanted to be an all-round
man of letters on the Eighteenth Century plan, which
allowed or commanded a man to write essay or poem, novel
or play, just as he pleases.' To that proclaimed taste for
liberty and variety Priestley has shaped the pattern of his
working life. From the first he has followed the wayward
course of a mind set free and of a hand skilled, as well as
ready, for all sorts of composition.

Between leaving Cambridge and the appearance of his
first large novel in 1929, he had been extremely active as
critic and essayist. Although there was then a much smaller
opportunity for such a talent in the early radio programmes,
a young writer and critic had a wider range of intelligent
reviews and magazines in which to place his work than has
the beginner today. These publications were mostly sustained
without profit and sometimes with private subsidy; but they
were there, and cheapness of production enabled them to
linger on in a market where present costs make the life of a
weekly impossible. So there was the scope; and in Priestley

there were the speed and the energy. As well as writing new books, he poured out reviews and essays, many of which were reprinted in book form; the best of the latter, in the author's own judgement, were reissued in his volume of *Self-Selected Essays* (1932).

As literary critic he contributed twice to the old-established series, 'The English Men of Letters', in which most of the great critics since the days of John Morley had been participants. Priestley's subjects were George Meredith (1926) and Thomas Love Peacock (1927). Another book which was much liked was *The English Comic Characters* (1925). Here was a subject rich and congenial.

Priestley has always retained a warm affection for drolls and, whether they were figures in a classical comedy or antic fellows of the contemporary stage, he has proved his own power to extract the essential juices of their humours and to explain and recommend the assorted flavours for a wide consumption and enjoyment. The business of criticism can be simply described as finding more in the arts for the advantage of others than those others can perceive for themselves. To communicating pleasures in this fruitful way of comment Priestley has added a well-maintained resolve to be a plain writer for the common reader; drollery is a public matter which has often been analysed by the precious for the admirers of allusive erudition. Nothing could be less Priestleyan than preciosity. He has explained that the natural scene can stir within his being a tincture of Thoreau's or of Wordsworth's ecstasy; and one of Wordsworth's best-known lines does, incidentally, sum up Priestley's response to good clowning and his communication of its pleasures. He enjoys this kind of joy and he would have it 'in widest commonalty spread'.

A potential and an excellent droll himself when in company—he has professed to being somewhat melancholy when alone—he composed in those years a portrait-gallery of the drolls to be seen in the theatres and music-halls. It was journalism of the best. To the routine of dramatic criticism, a severe tax on time and binding a man to hours and places, the libertarian Priestley naturally did not attach himself; but as an occasional theatrical writer and reviewer he has shown how shrewdly he could assess the players in all types of play.

During the nineteen-twenties the popularity of the personal essay was well maintained in English journalism. This form of writing did not, as a rule, seek to cope with the larger problems of life; it was not a deeply reflective and compact article, following the model of pithy sagacity set by Sir Francis Bacon; it was an amusing and discursive trifle on some topic of the day, social not sociological, or on any passing notion which had taken the 'writer's fancy. These 'middles', as they were called after their position in the middle of the paper, were usually non-political, being regarded as light relief from the 'leaders' on politics, and from the signed articles on foreign affairs. A periodical called *The Saturday Review* had established a high tradition of 'middle' writing when it had 'Max' (Sir Max Beerbohm) on its staff; his contributions were not limited to his dramatic criticism. It was for the same review that Priestley was the weekly essayist during some years at the beginning of his career.

There had been, and there still then remained, a notable group of essayists working on the journals and newspapers catering for a public which would appreciate writing of this quality and character. G. K. Chesterton's weekly piece for the *Daily News* earned a wide reputation and readership with its brilliant application of word-play and paradox to original thinking on all kinds of general habits and tendencies. Other first-rate artists of the essay were Hilaire Belloc, Maurice Baring, E. V. Lucas, Father Ronald Knox, Gerald Gould, and Robert Lynd. Their collected pieces were regularly printed in book-form. But the taste for this kind of writing dwindled. It was distinguished for its affable facility and felicity of style. It was labelled in book-sellers' lists as 'belles-lettres' and gradually 'belles-lettres' came to be almost a term of contempt. The younger readers of the reviews wanted more of realism in their favourite publications and less of the fanciful. They regarded these personal confessions and declarations of enjoyment as 'a bit bogus'. The essay, according to this view, was a display of stylistic prettiness and there was now no liking for anything pretty or for the essayist's cosiness of mood. Hard times had struck the nation; the fears and the facts of war were at hand. The benign essayist was 'out of this world'.

The American influence may have been at work, for the Americans had not liked the type of essay prevalent in English journalism. They considered themselves to be hard-bitten readers who wanted hard-biting writers. They asked of their journalism something tougher, more factual, and more combative than our suave 'middles'. English essayists wrote pleasantly of their pleasures, not angrily of their antipathies. Gradually those of the English 'weeklies' which did not die of poverty found life easier if they dropped the essay as a regular feature. The essayist had ceased to be a star-performer and an asset to circulation. The editors could not help noticing that the younger public now favoured the methods of *The New Yorker* which had no place for affability. So they began to seek something crisper and more contentious, to suit a generation which preferred the roughness of the wise-crack to the urbanity of the epigram. The new vogue was for a string of sharp, short commentary notes, signed, frequently, with a pseudonym.

Priestley came in towards the end of the essay-vogue and he was a vigorous as well as an entertaining contributor. He had an easy flow of humour and his range of topics was large. If the essay lost its place because of a reputation for prettiness and elegant prattle, it was not his fault. He always had something to say and said it without the tricks of the essayist's trade. This phase of his writing was, of course, closely personal, and he could be charmingly entertaining on such a subject as 'My Face and I', explaining that his features 'seemed to belong to a type of man that I dislike'.

But usually his essays had a base of keen social observation.

He described, for example, in one called 'The Pessimists', the loquacious melancholy of the young, a feature of English life that was as prominent in Shakespeare's youth as it is in our own. His theme was the hilarious world-condemnation uttered by his hearty and well-fed guests, obviously happy young people, on a glorious summer afternoon when it was bliss to be alive and 'Epicurus himself would not have disdained the situation'. Those who wish to examine the Priestley 'ego', with all its Yorkshire background and its London experience, its relish for music in the home as well as for the clowns in their various arenas, must read his essays; they will not find it difficult. In addition to *Self-Selected Essays* there has been another excellent volume called *Delights* (1949). In this volume he describes his many sources of self-entertainment or contented retrospect.

It was in this collection, too, that he published an essay called 'Too Simple?', which is valuable for the comprehension of all his work. He had been talking with a young critic whom he liked and respected, but whose values he did not accept. The younger man was surprised to find Priestley's thought and talk complex and subtle. 'Your writing', he added, 'always seems to me too simple.' To which Priestley naturally replied, 'I've spent years and years trying to make my writing simple. What you see as a fault, I regard as a virtue.' In his later comment in that essay he explained, with appropriate lucidity, the gulf between the clear communicators and the devotees of the difficult who had become influential with the young. The latter, he thought, were in revolt against 'the Mass Communication antics of their age'. They did not want to share things; they wanted to make their readers toil and sweat in the task of unravelling:

Difficulty (he wrote) was demanded; hence the vogue of Donne and Hopkins. Literature had to respond to something twisted, tormented, esoteric in their own secret natures. In all this there was no pose, and here their elders went wrong about them. They could be accused, not unjustly, of narrowness and arrogance, but not of insincerity. They were

desperately sincere in believing that the artist must hide from the crowd
behind a thicket of briars. They grew up terrified of the crowd, who, in
this new Mass Age, seemed to them to be threatening all decent values.
But I was born in the nineteenth century and my most impressionable
years were those just before 1914. Rightly or wrongly, I am not afraid
of the crowd. And art to me is not synonymous with introversion.

He then defended his 'simplicity' of expression and his
effort to achieve a prose style 'like an easy persuasive voice';
and he rightly added that to achieve such a style is much more
difficult than being difficult. The lucid writer does the hard
labour himself instead of leaving it to the reader. That
Priestley is far from a simpleton in thought is obvious to any
who follow him into the Fourth Dimension in his pursuit of
the truth about Time; but that he has mastered the quality
of persuasive clarity is no less plain to any reader of any of
his work.

Though suspicious of what are called Mass Communica-
tions, he has himself used them expertly. He can draft a
broadcast description of events to suit his own microphone
style and deliver it in the easy, persuasive manner of his ideal
for written prose. His spoken war-time 'Postscripts' of 1940
and after were for the most part reassurances and encourage-
ments, pictures of the national strength of character, technical skill, and stoutness of heart; there were tributes to the
simple country life continuing with its Home Guard duties,
and of the harassed urban existence with fire-watching after
long hours in the factory. When he urged a better time for
all as the reward of such ardours and endurances, he was
accused of being too political; this was the factious out-cry
of a faction rather than a general protest. Even those who
disliked his matter could not criticize the effectiveness of his
method in holding the ear of millions.

Before we turn to consider his novels and plays something
must be said of his use of travel. The literature of English
journeys, as well as of English Grand (and less Grand) Tours,
is a rich one. Priestley has added to it in his descriptions of
America and of England, descriptions which are also dis-

cussions; he uses the scenery for sitting back in speculation as well as for reporting while he moves. His *English Journey* (1934) was undertaken at the time of great industrial depression, and it has its outbursts of indignation as well as its vividness of reported observation. In 1955 he explored the world's 'newest rich' in the oil-fields of Texas while his wife, Jacquetta Hawkes, the archaeologist, was visiting the oldest America of the Pueblo Indians not far away. They published in 1955, *Journey Down a Rainbow*, a joint volume of letters written from their separate places of visitation. In Priestley's section there was an investigation of what he called 'Admass', the mixture of material prosperity and labour-saving techniques with fierce advertising pressures and continuous, ubiquitous mass-entertainment by the television which carries the advertisements and produces its own creed of success and of the Admass way of life. The man at the receiving end of all this believes that everything is opening out for the creation of ever more abounding plenty and pleasure; to Priestley it seemed that a great deal was closing in.

That is the kind of subject in treating which he is at his best. Journeys make some of us comatose; Priestley's mind vibrates with the engines. He cannot enter a railway station without entering on a train of thought. Sometimes he settles down to digest his travel. *Midnight on the Desert* (1937) was written in Arizona, and drew its contemplation from the sun-baked scenery which most of us associate with 'Westerns', while *Rail upon Godshill* (1939) took its title from the milder and moister landscape of the Isle of Wight. The dominant note of Priestley's philosophy is dislike of withdrawal and of the 'non-participation' advocated by Aldous Huxley. His criticism of most religions is that they are too narrowly ethical, too negligent of the real flame of life:

These last years (he wrote) I have been snowed under with pamphlets and booklets, Christian, Buddhist, Theosophical, New and Higher Thought, in which mere rejection or a negative attitude of mind is assumed to be the beginning of a spiritual life. You are asked to lead the existence of a ghost, a feeble and attenuated parody of a life . . . There is no place in their worlds, whether the material and fleshly here or the spiritual hereafter, for those battle-scarred giants of our race who have swung between passionate rebellion against the gods and agonies of pity and tenderness for their kind.

In Priestley's writing one is always coming up against the Radical, but certainly not the Roundhead Radical. If there is fire in him it is the Promethean fire, with its glow of conflict and its heating of the forge of thought. Though he likes his desert solitudes and his midnights under alien moons he does not stay there long. He could no more be a scholar-recluse than he could be a political reactionary. Participate he must. When he seems to have quietened down, there he is again in the drama of things. (The word 'drama' is Greek for a thing done, action not talk.) 'Enter on the Left, J. B. Priestley' is a stage-direction that we have come to look for and to welcome, for there will be comedy, as well as counsel, when he takes the dais. Active and activating he must be, but he will always be ready to laugh and, as he showed in many of his essays, he is well prepared to do some laughing a himself.

III

Priestley became fully established as a novelist when *The Good Companions* was published in 1929. Previously he had written two novels which proved that he could tell a good tale as well as write a good essay and make shrewd critical incursions into English literature. In addition to this pair, *Adam in Moonshine* (1927) and *Benighted* (1927) he had been a collaborator with his friend Hugh Walpole in a book called *Farthing Hall*, fiction based on interchange of letters, a device well used by Richardson. *The Good Companions* turned out to be what schoolboys call 'a smasher'. It was

twice the normal length; it had a Dickensian scope as well as
near-Dickensian vigour; it had a host of characters and a
swirl of movement. It was labelled by the classifiers as
'picaresque'. (The classifiers were in that case inaccurate
since 'picaresque' should mean a story about rogues and
vagabonds; Priestley's characters were chiefly strolling
players, but they were not rogues, of whose community
they were encounterers, but not representatives.) *The Good
Companions* was also a 'smasher' in its success. It was filmed
and dramatized with acceptance as well as selling vastly in
book form in many countries. It did not please thus greatly
because Priestley was writing down, but because he was
being very much himself and playing a strong hand.

The story begins in Bruddersford, essential Yorkshire,
drawn to the smoky life. There Mr. Oakroyd, essential
Bruddersford, unhappy in his home but able to be happy
almost anywhere else, is a carpenter who loses his job, leaves
his uncongenial wife and son, and finds adventures 'on t'
road'. He collides with two characters also flitting, Miss
Trant, a spinster who has left a prim country-house domesticity with her small car and a little capital, and Inigo
Jollifant, a young schoolmaster, too mercurial for an usher's
life and luckily owning a good hand at the piano and a
knack of writing catchy song-tunes.

These three not only run into each other; they also run
into a stranded concert-party. With Miss Trant's money,
Oakroyd's odd-jobbery, and Jollifant's musical talent they
give these penniless mummers and minstrels another chance.
The troup is renamed 'The Good Companions' and away
they all move 'on t' road' to bright weeks and black weeks,
to troubles and triumphs. They are likeable; their tale is
likeably told; and Priestley, who later on came to like the
acting profession much less, was then on very good terms
with his vagabond players and drew them with affection as
well as with authenticity.

The Good Companions, a book with a broad smile, became
a sore point with some critics later on, especially with the

type of critic who cannot forgive a great popular success. For the devotees of the difficult, who view the arts as privy things to be kept remote, here was the simplicity they deplored. The title had a ring of heartiness which they hated; the treatment did not probe the sub-conscious selves of distressed comedians and dredge up tragic squalor. One may surmise that those who were to dismiss the author as 'Jolly Jack Priestley, the Good Companion' had never done more than glance at the book, if they got as far as that. It was assumed, with characteristic intellectual snobbery, that any novelist who had achieved such wide popularity had been selling himself cheap. This was superficial nonsense.

The fictional journeys in the story have as much veracity of scene and incident as have Priestley's actual travels recorded in his *English Journey*. Hell-holes are not trans-muted into little bits of heaven. The survey of Bruddersford, with which the book opens, is Priestley at his best, and the unfolding panorama of small provincial towns with their mouldering theatres and concert halls, their drab hotels and more colourful bar-parlours, sustains the high level of social landscape. The pattern of the start, in which Oakroyd, Miss Trant, and Jollifant are all seen making their separate escapes into a larger world, is capitally designed. *The Good Companions* 'made' Priestley because he knew how to make human beings and to give them convincing background as well as how to make a large and lively story of cordial quality.

There was a prompt demonstration that the portrayal of provincial life on a generous scale could be followed with a no less generous canvas of London, both in its city and its suburban phases. *Angel Pavement* (1930) took its name from a typical side-street, an alley which housed, among others none too prosperous, a firm of timber-dealers, now in finan-cial trouble; a possible rescuer arrives and at first business improves, but this brassy, vociferous and whisky-swilling monster is, though apparently generous, looking after him-self while keeping on the safe side of the law. Nobody could say that in this case Priestley was cultivating an easy cheerfulness; the ending of the book is bleak indeed, for all the employees of the now broken timber firm are left in the air, the cold economic air of the nineteen-thirties, when unemployment cruelly swept the world.

In reading Priestley's work of that period one is constantly reminded of the great divergence between that decade and the years of the Second World War and after. The period of *Angel Pavement* was, for millions of people, grey with fear, fear of never getting a job, fear of losing that hard-held job, and fear of an existence without security and without hope. Little money might be earned, but it went a long way; one reads now with amazement at the salaries paid and what they bought. Yet the money might wither in a week. The temper of our epoch of Full Employment, with its jobs lightly abandoned and easily found, is radically different from that of the years of apprehension. To understand the strain of English life after the great industrial depression had set in it is a considerable help to have read Priestley's earlier novels as well as his *English Journey*.

Angel Pavement is, in fact, a London Journey through the chequered lives of accountants, secretaries, and office-boys as well as of harassed employers. The arrival and departure of the brash and masterful swindler provides little more plot than would fill out a long short story. But the author spreads himself in a way that suits his power of racy description. We share at some length in a catastrophic dinner-party at Earl's Court; we go to a women's hostel, to a Soho restaurant, 'determinedly foreign in a denationalized fashion, rather as though the League of Nations had invented it', and we penetrate the life of clerks in North London and Camden Town. It is a drab world, seen by a dashing colourist, a sad world seen by a great writer of comedy who is also a man of great compassion. *Angel Pavement* was a good companion to *The Good Companions*, because it turned the keys of different doors and drove with such insight into the work-a-day sufferings of the 'nine-to-six' existence when even that existence might suddenly cease to yield its meagre scraps of tea-and-bun catering.

The economic liberation which his immensely successful novel-writing brought to Priestley now enabled him to move widely. He sailed the Pacific as well as the Atlantic ocean, and out of his far-flung voyaging he wove a traveller's tale called *Faraway* (1932). This story was, in one way, ahead of its time since it concerned a search for uranium, needed then for radium and now, even more keenly, for its assistance in the creation of power, power to create and power also to annihilate. A curiously assorted party go in quest of a still uncharted island rich in the coveted mineral, and theirs is a long, strange, eventful voyage. The chief attraction of the book lies in its colour-prints of the islands and of the huge deserts of water between them. There are memorable passages about the fantastic beauty of the Marquesas and the weird, bare, sculpture-strewn plateau of Easter Island where a populous community once built ambitiously, made graven images on a gigantic scale, and then vanished in a sudden, mysterious doom. In this book the island-studded oceans overflow the characters, but Priestley makes shrewd use of the ironies implied. Nature is at its grandest among the coral reefs, but man is engaged in running night-clubs proper to a third-rate city life, or peddling trashy gewgaws to the perhaps once noble savage.

After this trio of 'out-size' novels Priestley put much of his quenchless energy into the theatre, and since then, with one exception, his novels have been shorter and crisper. The exception was *Festival at Farbridge* (1951), a piece for the occasion since it was written to greet the many junketings of that Festival Year. It described with plentiful humour the agonized efforts to supply joy to order in a sombre and contentious Midland town into which revelry could only be imported with perseverance and perplexity. In this case Priestley seemed to be less fluent than before; there is much good laughter to be had from his Farbridge and its Festival capers, but the author appears to be labouring at times.

The shorter novels are so numerous that they cannot be discussed in detail. In most cases Priestley drew on immediate scenes and happenings, the war-time 'black-out' and the great drive in the war-factories, the coming of demobilization and release, and the readjustments to a new economy. One of the best of them is called *Bright Day* (1946). The first hundred pages describe a youngster's life in Bruddersford before the Great Wars came and put their darkness on a massacred and mourning world. There were long hours and dull jobs, but there were streets lit-up at closing-time, and eyes that lit up too when there was a party to be joined. The description of Boxing Day at Mr. Ackworth's is wonderful comedy. Written with tenderness as well as gusto, it derides none of the parlour fun unkindly and it responds with communicable friendliness to the cult of 'good stuff' in food and drink and music-making. It was Yorkshire being Yorkshire, and yet escaping from Yorkshire with its home-made arts. 'With one clean stroke, as clean as his opening phrases, Leaton cut straight through the insurance business, the wool business, Bruddersford, and the twentieth century, straight through to the eighteenth century and Johann Sebastian Bach!' And then, the lad with belly and senses slaked, goes out into the street with the girls for company, through the thickening snow and the blanket of the night, 'aglow with the immense vague dreams of youth'. His world, in the snow and the darkness, 'was opening like a flower'. The good stuff of conviviality and beauty and human character is here recorded in writing better than good.

Because Priestley excels in description, he has been criticized as reporting, not creating. He is thus made a victim of his own virtue, since nobody denies that he is a superb recorder, able to seize in words the essentials of any place or community through which he may, perhaps hurriedly, have passed. His speed of observation is equalled by his sureness in choice of the right phrase. But because he has such readiness in making the report, it is absurd to overlook the creation of character in which he shows no less capacity. I have said that in *Faraway* the richly painted oceans submerged the persons of the story, yet more than one head is conspicuous above the waters, most notably that of the traveller called Ramsbottom, a Lancashire businessman who joins the expedition, a coarse but solid and loyal piece of humanity, greedy but avid for quality. Passionate for 'good stuff', he is a decent lump of good stuff himself, crude in his merits but genuine in his generosity. It is too easy, just because the Priestley background is always vividly authentic, to overlook the authenticity of the people in front of it.

In his *Midnight on the Desert* Priestley has replied to those critics who, having found this 'reporter' label, gummed it on mechanically:

They were not intending to be complimentary; the inference was that reporting was my level. They may well be right when they hint that the higher, grander, subtler forms of imaginative writing are quite beyond me; I have never made any great claims for my fiction, beyond protesting once or twice that there might be a little more in it than met the top-speed reviewer's eye, and that because I once wrote one jolly, hearty, popular novel it doesn't follow that everything I have written since is exactly the same.

He then explained that, while in the American desert, he was writing of the London scene:

A man in Arizona who attempts to describe with some wealth of detail what it feels like to be a waitress or a parlourmaid in London, using not one single note, may be a good, bad, or indifferent novelist, but he will certainly not be much of a reporter. He has removed himself far from the scene; he has not prepared himself to describe it and only by a fairly violent use of his imagination can he identify himself with characters so entirely different from himself. If this is reporting, I no longer understand the English language.

The obvious reply to the accusation of 'mere reporting' lies in Priestley's ability to write plays. There can be no background word-painting here. (Shaw did provide this with his immensely detailed descriptions of scene and character, but Priestley did not follow that example.) A play lives by its characters and its dialogue; of course individual people known and observed can be the basis of characterization in a play as in a book. But there can be no recourse to long accounts of what the people look like and do. They must live by the words invented for them and conveyed in dialogue at a far shorter length than the novelist employs. Drama cannot spread itself in verbal panorama; it is concentrated and compact. It cannot live without imagining; the reporter, however gifted, is useless in that form of writing. It is only fair to Priestley to consider the number of others who have been masters of both narrative and play-building. In our own theatre there is Somerset Maugham. John Galsworthy began with two or three first-rate plays, but his later output was disappointing and he will be remembered for his novels. Priestley has been exceptionally eager and able to write for his readers and for the theatre public simultaneously. To guess about an artist's survival is always rash, but one may risk a surmise that future generations will be reviving the best of his plays more frequently than reading the best of his novels.

IV

Priestley's work for the stage began with a collaboration; he was assisted by that ever-ready adapter and ally of the novelist turned dramatist, Edward Knoblock, who had done so much for Arnold Bennett in the theatre. Thus the large and largely popular story of *The Good Companions* was made into a play with music, the airs being provided by Richard Addinsell. Produced in May 1931, it ran for nearly a year. This successful follow-up of a fictional success was satisfying, but it was far from sufficing Priestley's theatrical ambitions or determining their scope.

Really there can have been little need of Knoblock's ministrations, for Priestley had it in him from the start to be a playwright, and his approach to this new phase of his work was characteristic in the swiftness of grip upon the new medium. He had foreseen that, since he was well-known as a novelist, it would be generally expected that he would write the kind of plays expected of novelists, loosely constructed stories with a tiresome number of scene-changes, or else an ill-packed bundle of ideas. So he began by demonstrating that he could write in as tight and economical a dramatic form as any established technician of the craft. *Dangerous Corner* (1932) had the classical unities of time, place and theme: its swiftly moving record of an impending family disaster had all the conflict and suspense that have ever been recommended in the 'How-to-write-a-play' textbooks. Priestley the novelist proved at one stroke that the manufacturers of the well-made play had nothing to teach him.

With this point made, he could proceed to larger matters and to a more personal and subtle form of theatrical expression. It is an essential part of Priestley's character that he is eager to be in the middle of things, active in the affairs and administration of life as well as in the recording and valuation of its events. (Standing as an Independent, he very nearly became Member of Parliament for Cambridge University in 1945—before University representation had been abolished.) He is the opposite of the detached and disengaged author who works in pacific isolation and sends the result of his desk-work to his agent, publisher, or manager, to arrange the 'promotion' of it. In the theatre the 'promotion' entails vitally important decisions on casting and production. Priestley, so far from being aloof, has readily been involved and has thought it only proper that those who make money in the theatre should be ready, if they have funds in hand, to plough them back into this same needy soil: that is a generous policy very rarely adopted by those who have done well out of play-royalties. Later on, for example, he was to be a backer of a venture called the London Masque Theatre which sponsored some very interesting productions of plays, new and old, with no reward for the investment made.

After *Dangerous Corner*, which, incidentally, might well be the title of a play about theatrical finance, he became associated with the management of the Duchess Theatre, a small and most suitable house for the intimate and realistic kind of play which he was now going to write. He began with a broad comedy, *Laburnum Grove* (1934), of which more will be said later. Typical of this period of Priestley's theatre work was its successor, *Eden End* (1934). For this piece he drew on the Yorkshire background, always likely to yield his best portrayal of character, his saltiest humour, and his ripest humanity of touch. He took his audience to a country doctor's home; hither came the daughter who had gone out to be a victorious actress, the pride of the family. She had returned with no laurels, but with an amusing but unhelpful husband. A small play about small people, it was large in balanced sympathy, and as moving as it was entertaining. Domesticity in provincial surroundings was also the theme of another Duchess Theatre play, *Time and the Conways* (1937). Into this, as the title implies, Priestley had injected his deep interest in the nature, perhaps the illusory nature, of the sequence of temporal events. Can it be that the future has already been lived in human experience? With such notions applied to the Conways in their life between the wars, the dramatist used the flash-forward, instead of the usual flash-back, in order to show, in poignant prophecy, how the hopes and dreams of a happy family may turn to sadness and chagrin and how the flowers of their fancies may be fading even when they seem to be blossoming. The veracity of the family portraits, young and old, was irresistible.

With his Conways, as with his Kirbys of *Eden End*, Priestley showed his close and compassionate understanding of the domestic tensions between members of the same generation as well as between parents and children. To show how the rhythm and security of life behind four ordinary walls may suffer disruption and pass from expectation to dismay was the object, but here was a domestic and rather doleful philosophy with cheerfulness obstinately breaking in. In the case of *The Linden Tree* (1948) there was a similar success of method and a much greater success of box-office. In this piece a resolute and ageing Professor at a Redbrick University was seen at odds with the policy and personnel of the changing academic life, and also with the views and activities of his now adult children. Such representatives of Priestley's early work in the theatre, together with *Cornelius* (1935) a study of a failure in business, are plays of the workaday world, factual in method of composition, plausible in plot, mirrored versions of what is going on in homes and offices by the myriad. They contain the essentials of the human comedy, but reach beyond it to the sting and sombreness of disenchantments, even of despairs. There is humour on the hearth. But even the ingle-nook can be a dangerous corner. The hearth is warming a house which has its chilly share of heartbreak.

Some people hold the view—and it is a very reasonable view—that Priestley is at his best in plays of this kind, realistic in style, cordial in their comedy, sympathetic in mood, and written with an urgency of feeling that has its tragic implications. But he himself became impatient with the hum-drum and the natural. Realism in the arts has been dismissed as 'the rags and tatters of pretended fact', and Priestley has certainly felt at times that he was in no mood to stay in the rag-trade. He would not be limited by the chatter and the scenery of realism or cabined by the confines of the immediately perceptible world.

One of the earlier ventures in escape from this sense of imprisonment by the actual and factual was the writing of *Johnson over Jordan* (1939). This play carries a likeable specimen of the Average Sensual Man through his yearnings, dreams, and frustrations and lifts him to the verge of eternity. The dramatic method employed was more episodic and dispersed than that of the naturalistic drama. Expressionism, a foolish and unhelpful term since all art is expression of something in some way, is a name loosely applied to such a form of play-writing, and the word appears to frighten both the British public and the British critics. There may be a change coming, but during the first half of the twentieth century British playgoers were doggedly faithful to the well-told story, set in recognizable surroundings. The drama which seeks to live upon imagination more than upon observation, thus reaching above the norma laughter of accepted comedy or the lustier chortle of routine farce, starts under handicap. It is significant that *The Linden Tree* has, with its realism, given Priestley far his longest London run. We may conclude that if Johnson's tale had been told with less fantasy, it might have had more favour. As it was, it had its passionate supporters, but they were not numerous enough. In any case 1939 was a difficult year, menaced by the near-certainty of war to come, a year better for trivial entertainment than for the dramatizing of first and last things and matters of high moment.

To mention the British rejection of Expressionist or Surrealist theatre is not to support or defend the public taste. It is merely to explain the difficulties encountered by any British dramatist who is resolved to risk that rejection, and to raise the sights of his theatrical workmanship. Posterity may allot to *Johnson over Jordan* a premier place among Priestley's copious and widely varied compositions for the stage. He himself would probably wish that to be so, for he has repeatedly stated his discontent with the limitations of the immediately probable story realistically presented. The urge to get outside the domestic interiors, in which he had moved with such a sureness of step, and to stride out more spaciously grew, instead of diminishing, with the years. Priestley has no interest in self-repetition and would rather risk a fall by vaulting ambitiously than continue securely in doing yet again what he has already done extremely well. But with the majority of play-goers it has been the case that not strangeness but familiarity breeds content.

At the same time Priestley has never lost his relish of drollery and his power to create absurdity as well as to enjoy it. A considerable section of his dramatic writing has been deliberately aimed at the public who come for a good laugh. Some of this work was not meant to be important or enduring and was composed for special circumstances. *How Are They At Home?* was written in 1944 for Ensa companies to perform for the Services overseas. *Good Night, Children* (1942) was a joke aimed at the radio of that period. Priestley has suggested that the war-time public were so much dependent on broadcasting that they found his mockery a trifle painful.

In one of the prefaces to his volumes of Collected Plays he has distinguished between High, Light, and Broad Comedy. High Comedy he regards as unpopular with British writers and public, but appealing with particular force to Latin and Central European audiences: our preference, especially among the wealthier play-goers, he allots to Light Comedy, since it provides admirable opportunities to skilled star-performers in this line, and of these the British Theatre has been sufficiently productive. Of late there has been a growing reliance on the players with a 'box-office name', and the combination of a slick example of Light Comedy with one or two of these 'names' is so powerful that managers naturally prefer to put their money on this type of article:

My own choice (he wrote) is Broad Comedy, which is stronger in situation than Light Comedy, and more frankly farcical and less austerely intellectual than High Comedy. It is, I believe, peculiarly suitable to the English temperament and, as I consider that I possess a fairly thick slab of this temperament, it is the field of comedy in which I have chosen to work.

And in the chosen field he did, intermittently, work to very good effect. His one piece produced in London in 1955, *Mr. Kettle and Mrs. Moon*, was of this category, a broadly humorous picture of respectability in revolt, with a bank manager tossing his bowler over the windmill.

Priestley began his connection with the Duchess Theatre by giving it *Laburnum Grove*, Broad Comedy in a suburban

setting. Another much welcomed essay in this vein was
When We Are Married (1938). The plot, he has stated, is
nonsensical, but the characters are authentic: he was drawing
on the Yorkshire types whose varieties of gravity and levity
he had absorbed as a boy; in this piece he had rare fun with
the petty potentates of Local Government and their wives,
and with a tippling photographer who drifts in. When an
excellent actor, Frank Pettingell, well suited to the part, was
out of the cast, Priestley took over the role himself and, as he
has said, 'I did some sort of acting, about which I have
boasted ever since'. He could manage, and enjoy, a personal
appearance and he could hold his own with the 'regulars'.
Like Charles Dickens, who was a gifted actor, Priestley
could have made a very good living as a comedian had he
become exasperated with the writing of rich comedy parts
for 'the profession'. The vitality, so abundant in the abun-
dance of his writing, overflows in the admirable mimicry
and caricature with which he can illustrate an anecdote and
enliven company. Broad Comedy, again, in life as in letters.

But, though liking the Broad and finding a rewarding
welcome for his provision of it, he was here, as elsewhere,
impatient of the groove. Various means of varying the
playhouse patterns and formulae were explored. There was
Bees on the Boatdeck (1936), an attempt to mingle political
and economic satire with a briskly comical, even farcical,
plot. It did not greatly please: the British playgoer is shy of
politics in the theatre and, though the distressing industrial
conditions of the 1930's made Priestley's picture of a wasting
economy and wasteful misuse of human ability sharply
relevant, there was some reluctance to take the instruction
in the midst of the amusement.

V

This brings one to the common accusation that Priestley
has been too much a political preacher, bringing to the stage
matters better suited to the pamphlet or the propagandist

volume. During the war he was greatly moved by the tremendous efforts and endurances made by the anonymous millions, many of whom had no reason to thank their country for its treatment of unemployment and destitution during the previous decade. He had every right, as a generous-minded man, to feel, speak and write as he did and to urge a broader conception of social justice. If he did bring opinions on social justice into some of his plays, he was but doing, with a more workmanlike technique, what Shaw had done in his youth and was constantly doing in his old age. It is a deplorably non-adult view of the theatre's function that rules out as non-theatrical any dramatic discussion of problems which are not purely personal.

Shaw had railed against the sensual romanticism which condemned actors and actresses to be for ever lovers or concerned with that most tedious and ubiquitous of themes, clandestine adultery. Granville-Barker and Galsworthy had been ready, and even willing, to plead causes and to make the stage a dais for the presentation of the larger conflicts of public life. Priestley, in *They Came To a City* (1944) and *Home Is To-morrow* (1949), brought news and views of the great world-changes and fresh outlooks into the routine-bound market of war-time and after-war entertainment. If he had done nothing else but advance his own doctrine, there might have been ground for complaint. But he also brought his stage-sense and his dexterity in drawing character into any pronouncement of a creed, and *They Came To a City* had a long run in the middle of the war, perhaps despite, rather than because of, its element of political persuasion. A playwright with no tincture of doctrine in his plays can win enormous successes by his craft in the staging of a story and by his portrayal of personal relations. Somerset Maugham and Terence Rattigan have both done so. But Theatre Street should be the site of many mansions and it would be a sad business if there were to be no corner in the huge industry of entertainment for the stimulation of the minority who do not leave all civic interests at home when they go to be entertained. All play and no work can make dull boys of Tom, Dick, and Harry.

But the number of Priestley's 'preachments' has been relatively small when matched with the frequency and fertility of his other contributions to the theatre. If sexual relations be deemed the most amusing or exciting of all subjects (and plainly the majority of play-goers in the commercial theatre think it is), Priestley has given them a large helping of their favourite fare. In doing so, his restless and inventive talents have been engaged on novel lines. *Ever Since Paradise*, for example, written in 1939 but not staged until 1946, used a strikingly fresh method of dealing with the dilemma of all Adams and all Eves since man and woman first loved and quarrelled, desired and differed and despaired. It might be called a charade with musical accompaniment. It did not triumph in London, where conservative criticism and the popularity of the ordinary lounge-hall setting and naturalistic performance, worked against it. But it has had wide welcome on the Continent.

In it there are only six characters, and two of them are engaged as commentators and pianists, rendering words and music appropriate to the changing moods in the story of a marriage. A mature married couple discuss and are involved in the mating and separation of a younger couple, and this can only be done by frequent changes of place and time and by the intervention of the elders in various wigs and costumes. There is no pretence that the wigs are really hair, and the rejection of the pretences of realism may have disturbed the enemies of innovation. The word charade has been used, and Priestley accepts it with the addition that it was very carefully written. Its production on the stage, for which he himself was largely responsible, obviously involved more detailed manœuvring and timing than would a comedy written and presented on conventional lines. To have undertaken this arduous work in planning and rehearsing the complicated simplicity of the piece was evidence of the dramatist's affection for it, and of his faith that it seemed to create a new and valuable relationship between players and audience.

The soaring costs of production in an inflationary period so much affected the making and marketing of books that their prices had to be much increased, though not in proportion to the rising cost of many other commodities. In the theatre, with its need for ever more expensive costumes and stage-labour, the economic problem became even more distracting. Priestley's experience of management and all its worries made him keenly aware of the necessity for evading all unnecessary charges. Theatre-rents were a mounting burden: so were salaries and wages; so, most of all, were the expenses of production and of the provision of scenery.

While in America in the autumn of 1951 he appreciated the extraordinary success which came to an experiment made by some leading actors, now chiefly film-actors, Charles Laughton, Charles Boyer, and Sir Cedric Hardwicke. This was achieved by a dramatic reading of Shaw's *Don Juan in Hell*, and here, plainly, was a suggestion for a new and more economical method of reaching the public with the spoken word and with actors' personality added. Accordingly, in collaboration with Jacquetta Hawkes, he wrote and organized performances of *Dragon's Mouth*, described as 'a dramatic quartet'. The four players learned and did not read their parts: but they were more or less static in front of a very simple setting. This new model differed from the stage-play in that it was highly mobile and could be toured in halls, thus avoiding the difficulty and cost of getting ordinary theatrical accommodation. Artistically it brought back rhetoric to the actors' lips, for the discussion carried on by the four characters was not chopped up into the fragmentary and often muttered style of the dialogue in realistic plays. Radio, in Priestley's opinion, had given people a taste for talk about conflicting ideas: *Dragon's Mouth* was to meet that taste with something larger, something more varied, now oratorical and now conversational; and something warmed with the personality of actors there in person, actors with emotions to portray as well as ideas to deliver.

In this 'quartet' two men and two women of different types, representing Jung's four functions of Thought, Feeling, Sensation and Intuition, were seen under threat of immediate death, first of death for all four and then of death for one. They can do nothing to save themselves: there is time for talk, and the debate ranges over the nature and relations of the sexes and the nature and capacity of mankind in its various forms of self-fulfilment. There are many fine passages of well-phrased speculation, and the players engaged mastered their enormous parts and spoke them well. There was a tour of provincial halls and there was a season at the huge Winter Garden Theatre in London in the summer of 1952. In the opinion of those receptive to experiment in the theatre, there was much value in this flexible form of presentation which could be accommodated (with microphones) to any kind of building. This Platform Theatre, which attracted and delighted much good listening, was something, as was claimed, to set against the standardization of Television. But experiments have to be followed up. The first time out is bound to reveal difficulties and the public has to be made aware of what is going on.

If this new model was to be given further chances, it needed further practice and the services of skilled 'promotion'. Priestley knew that, but he is not a follower-up. Explaining how he undertook the experiment with *Dragon's Mouth* he wrote, 'I am an impatient man, always have been and now, it seems, always will be. I cannot bear waiting long for anything good to happen. I have never been able, as superior beings are able, to plan far ahead, to settle today what I shall be doing in two or three years' time. I rush at anything—even work.' Having hurried into their drama of the dais with gusto, Priestley and Jacquetta Hawkes did not plod on with Platform Theatre, and they have had no imitators, except in so far as small groups produce plays, sometimes plays of discussion, in the simplest kind of setting and often with the audience circled about an arena-stage. *Dragon's Mouth*, as presented at the Winter Garden, was far from being 'Theatre-in-the-Round', which was beginning to acquire a vogue among the groups. But since it is available for use in all forms of architecture, it can be called Theatre Elastic. As the number of ordinary theatres has sadly diminished in the country owing to the commercial value of their sites and the competitive pressure of Television, the need for such elasticity is obvious, and the *Dragon's Mouth* experiment should have been valuable in showing what can be done to find new premises for a new style of play-craft.

No major piece of Priestley's followed it on the English stage: but his impatience has within it a patience of his own. Amid disappointments and delays he is always ready to grumble, but never to give in. Delays have to be stressed, because the business of selecting, casting, and producing plays is often infuriatingly slow. Perhaps all depends on getting a certain well-liked actor: and that actor, having loosely agreed, begins to doubt and then, with a big film-contract calling, resolves to depart. With the writing and issuing of books there are not these complications and exasperations. It is a fair interpretation of Priestley's temperament that he has been partly stage-struck most of his life. He has had his consolations when the best of his writing was well played and well received, and he has had his spells of angry disappointment, when the criticisms seemed shallow and spiteful and the public slow and crass. Since he could always have filled his time profitably as a novelist and journalist, with much less risk of hard labour sometimes ill-rewarded, his loyalty to the theatre has been the more remarkable.

Priestley's work, especially his dramatic work, has found much admiration outside Britain, and in his most recent years some plays of his have had their first production abroad. This was the case with *Take the Fool Away*, first acted in Vienna in 1956. This picture of a clown at large and bewildered in a highly mechanized and authoritarian society, had an enthusiastic reception. The Scandinavian and Central European countries have been especially eager for his writing.

There was a lessening of devotion to theatrical practice during the last half of the nineteen-fifties; the conditions of a playwright's occupation were being found increasingly vexatious. In his fascinating book of reminiscences, *Margin Released* (1962), of which more will be said later, he deplored the Monte Carlo, hit-or-miss finance and the 'peculiar atmosphere of giddiness and silliness that seems to have robbed the English-speaking Theatre of any sensible continuing tradition'. In this 'over-heated atmosphere of dazzling successes and shameful flop, you are a wonder-man in October, a pretentious clown in March, you are in, you are out. . . . No competent English or American playwright is as good or as bad as managers, theatrical press, and public say he is. They are playing roulette with him.'

But there was reflection on the theatre in a sizeable essay on *The Art of the Dramatist* (1957). In this Priestley maintained that any Great Theatre to come would not be created and dominated by the star actor with his box-office personality, the powerful director with his new interpretations, or the master-showman with his restless pursuit of the 'smash hit'. The senior partner must be the dramatist. This was argued with reference to the great flowerings of drama which, at various periods, have been planted and fertilized by the word written for the speaker, with the word as the principal source of the world's recurrent bursts of theatrical vitality.

Priestley did, however, come back as an adapting dramatist in 1963 when he collaborated with Iris Murdoch in turning her strangely sinister and much-discussed novel *A Severed Head* into a neatly-contrived comedy of sexual manœuvre. First produced at the Bristol Old Vic, it came to the Criterion Theatre in London and had a very long run. There was something cold and rather cruel in the play's setting to partners; there was lechery made amusing but without

affection and with little of the warmth of Priestley's usual
approach to life. But it evidently suited the mood of the
time. As Priestley himself explained in the conclusion to
Literature and Western Man (1960) 'in this atomic age, sure of
nothing but sex . . . we are now piling on to sex the whole
gigantic load of our increasing dissatisfactions, our despair,
a load far greater than it can take.'

The familiar and sometimes unjustified phrase, a life-work,
can be fairly applied to the great volume just mentioned.
Authors are often asked how long it has taken them to write
a book; some are the product of a swift thought and immediate composition. But for the great achievement the
answer well may be, 'I have been writing it all my life'.
Priestley set out to chronicle and evaluate the literature and
drama of Europe and the United States from the invention
of the printing-press to the outbreak of the Second World
War. Such a task could not have been attempted without
rapid and voracious reading since boyhood. It is astonishing
that anybody could have read so much and no less astonishing that so much could have been described and analysed
within the compass of one book. It is one of Priestley's
peculiar and valuable gifts to be able to condense without
serious omissions. He proved that in his brief text to an
illustrated life of Charles Dickens (1961). There he managed
to say in twenty thousand words |more than others could
say with five times that space at their disposal. All that the
average reader needs for an understanding of Dickens's inner
conflicts amid the the pressures of his immensely busy public
life is there set out with as much brevity as perception.

Literature and Western Man is divided into five sections.
Part One, 'The Golden Globe', relates the writers to the new
worlds discovered on the map and in the mind at the end of
the Middle Ages. As major figures of that epoch and particularly discussed are Shakespeare and Cervantes. Then comes
'The Order'd Garden', in which the eighteenth century's
mental patterns are traced in their variety of form and
texture. In 'Shadows of the Moon' the romantic reaction

against formalism is the theme. In 'The Broken Web' we meet the fine confusion of the huge Victorian output. 'The web is vast, for there is now far more writing that can fairly be called literature than there was in the earlier ages, but it has been stretched so hard in many directions that it is broken.' The writers of the time are seen as living on the surface of the new industrialized and mechanized society and delving in their special directions below that massive muddle. The fifth section is devoted to 'The Moderns', who were the products and the critics of a society 'rapidly cutting itself loose from the past or at least appearing to do so, busy changing everything that could be changed'.

Some facts about the authors are given and then comment of a never sourly critical kind. Each writer is fairly viewed in the light of his intentions and not scolded for having wrong intentions. Priestley is not ruling out what he dislikes; he is looking into all forms of authorship and all moods of the authors to discover their achievement in their own way of working. Psychological analysis accompanies examination of technique, and the insistence on the hidden emotional stresses is sometimes carried so far as to leave the rational element in creative work under-valued. But this is a tremendous survey with its ample service of the student as well as of the general reader. Priestley disclaims scholarship, but that quality, in its best and most discerning form, is there. Moreover, it is communicated with ease and lucidity, as well as with a width of sympathy extended to authors not wholly congenial to the critic. No patch of fog obscures this huge literary landscape. The man who has read so keenly and dispersedly is always supremely readable. The book has been translated into four foreign languages and extensively read in Britain and America.

Margin Released, which appeared two years later, is loosely autobiographical and lights up three sections of Priestley's life. There is the Bradford boyhood with its happy evasions of an office routine and its adventures of the young mind at large. There follows his share in and fortunately safe emergence from the monstrous slaughter of the first World War; here is narrative, sometimes humorous, always without self-pity, and with comment fired by a passionate indignation at the follies in high places. It is a subject that Priestley had hitherto kept buried in his mind; he had not written of those years before. The memories now released are characteristically vivid and poignant.

The final section follows the ardours and endurances of Priestley the journalist, broadcaster, novelist and dramatist, with some notable portraiture of others prominent in these occupations; one might call this part of the book a light supplement added to *Literature and Western Man*, at least on the English side of that major operation. Again there is a large generosity for his fellow-authors combined with resentment for the conditions of their labour, especially in the theatre. There is justice done, for example, to Hugh Walpole whose one-time popularity and relish of being well-regarded made unforgiving enemies and detractors who overlooked the best of his writing. Priestley does not remain uncritical of his friends at work in this often jarring and fractious society of writers; he knows their failures as well as their merits and is candid about his own. He restores balance where that is needed and remembers what others too easily forget amid the turbid scramble of competitive publishing and the ups-and-downs of reputation in the arts.

Novel writing continued, but not on the grand scale of the early fiction. *Saturn Over the Water* (1961) mingled the power-politics and international intrigue of the Atom Bomb Age with some striking descriptions of travel far and wide. *Sir Michael and Sir George* (1964) is a satirical comedy about two rival Arts Councils. During 1963 much time and thought were given to *Man and Time*, which was to be published in the following year. Here is another reversion, in a large illustrated book, to Priestley's constant subject of reflection, man's relations with time and how he has measured and thought about it. His own speculations on its mystery are added to those of others. He had in a B.B.C.

'Monitor' programme invited viewers to send him accounts of unusual time experiences and there was a vast response, especially about pre-cognitive dreams, and examining these proved to be a task as rewarding as it was great.

It is useless to speculate on what Priestley will do next. He is as unpredictable as he is unwearying. Age does not diminish this activity. He is always anxious to follow new ideas into new countries of the mind and he has ample energy for that pursuit. He has certainly proved himself to be one of the most versatile, as well as one of the most vivid, of British authors. A film-script or a libretto for an opera are as readily undertaken as a new book or play. This may have cost him the esteem of those critics who think, despite so many famous examples to the contrary, that speed of output and wide range of creation must be suspect and that quality is incompatible with quantity. But Priestley is not one to be deflated or deflected by that kind of belittlement.

For the kind of criticism that delights in tracing literary influences, Priestley is a bad subject. All his life he has read widely and absorbed rapidly; but other writers' ideas and methods, however much appreciated, may affect, but do not dominate, his own. A man of such various gifts and such multifarious practice in the arts belongs to no 'school'. He creates, and recreates, in his own way. Classifications do not contain him. He is immensely, unquenchably, himself.

J. B. PRIESTLEY

A Select Bibliography

(Place of publication London, unless stated otherwise)

Collected Works:

THE COLLECTED EDITION (in course of publication).

THE POPULAR EDITION OF THE NOVELS (in course of publication).

THE PLAYS (in course of publication).

Selected Works:

SELF SELECTED ESSAYS (1932)
—included in *The Collected Edition.*

FOUR IN HAND (1934)

—containing *Adam in Moonshine, Laburnum Grove, The Roundabout* and a selection of criticism, travel and essays.

GOING UP (1950)
—stories and sketches, published by Pan Books.

THE PRIESTLEY COMPANION (1951)
—a Selection, with an Introduction by Ivor Brown.

Collections of Plays:

TWO TIME PLAYS (1937)
—containing *Time and the Conways* and *I have been Here Before.*

THREE PLAYS (1943)
—containing *Music at Night, The Long Mirror* and *They came to a City.*

FOUR PLAYS (1944)
—*Three Plays,* 1943, with *Desert Highway.*

THREE COMEDIES (1945)
—containing *Goodnight, Children, The Golden Fleece* and *How are they at home?*

THREE TIME PLAYS (1947)
—*Two Time Plays,* 1937, with *Dangerous Corner.*

Separate Works:

THE CHAPMAN OF RHYMES (1918). *Verse*

BRIEF DIVERSIONS. Cambridge (1922). *Miscellany*
—includes parodies, epigrams, light essays, etc.

PAPERS FROM LILLIPUT. Cambridge (1922). *Sketches*

I FOR ONE (1923). *Essays*

FIGURES IN MODERN LITERATURE (1924). *Criticism*

THE ENGLISH COMIC CHARACTERS (1925). *Criticism*

GEORGE MEREDITH (1926). *Criticism*
—in the English Men of Letters series.

TALKING (1926). *Essays*
—including items contributed to the *Saturday Review*.

ADAM IN MOONSHINE (1927). *Novel*

OPEN HOUSE (1927). *Essays*
—including items contributed to the *Saturday Review*.

THOMAS LOVE PEACOCK (1927). *Criticism*
—in the English Men of Letters Series.

BENIGHTED (1927). *Novel*

THE ENGLISH NOVEL (1927). *Criticism*

APES AND ANGELS (1928). *Essays*
—including items contributed to the *Saturday Review*.

FARTHING HILL (1929). *Fiction*
—in collaboration with Hugh Walpole.

ENGLISH HUMOUR (1929). *Criticism*

THE GOOD COMPANIONS (1929). *Novel*
—dramatized with E. Knoblock, 1931.

THE BALCONINNY (1929). *Essays*
—including items contributed to the *Week End Review*.

THE TOWN MAYOR OF MIRAUCOURT (1930). *Short Story*

ANGEL PAVEMENT (1930). *Novel*

DANGEROUS CORNER (1932). *Drama*

FARAWAY (1932). *Novel*

WONDER HERO (1933). *Novel*

THE ROUNDABOUT (1933). *Drama*

ALBERT GOES THROUGH (1933). *Story*

LABURNUM GROVE (1934). *Drama*

ENGLISH JOURNEY (1934). *Description*

EDEN END (1934). *Drama*

DUET IN FLOODLIGHT (1935). *Drama*

CORNELIUS (1935). *Drama*

SPRING TIDE (1936). *Drama*
—the original edition was published as by George Billam and Peter Goldsmith, the latter being a pseudonym for J. B. Priestley.

BEES ON THE BOAT DECK (1936). *Drama*

THEY WALK IN THE CITY (1936). *Novel*

MIDNIGHT ON THE DESERT (1937). *Autobiography*

TIME AND THE CONWAYS (1937). *Drama*

MYSTERY OF GREENFINGERS (1937). *Drama*

I HAVE BEEN HERE BEFORE (1937). *Drama*

PEOPLE AT SEA (1937). *Drama*

THE DOOMSDAY MEN (1938). *Novel*

WHEN WE ARE MARRIED (1938). *Drama*

JOHNSON OVER JORDAN (1939). *Drama*

RAIN UPON GODSHILL (1939). *Autobiography*

LET THE PEOPLE SING (1939). *Novel*

THE LONG MIRROR (1940). *Drama*

POSTSCRIPTS (1940). *Broadcast talks*
—talks broadcast during some of the darkest hours in the Second World War.

OUT OF THE PEOPLE (1941). *Commentary*
—war-time political papers.

GOODNIGHT, CHILDREN (1942). *Drama*

BLACK-OUT IN GRETLEY (1942). *Story*

DAYLIGHT ON SATURDAY (1943). *Novel*

THE MAN-POWER STORY (1943). *Commentary*
—a factual statement of the war-time use of manpower. Written for the Ministry of Labour.

BRITISH WOMEN GO TO WAR (1943). *Sociology*

DESERT HIGHWAY (1944). *Drama*

HOW ARE THEY AT HOME? (1944). *Drama*

THEY CAME TO A CITY (1944). *Drama*

THREE MEN IN NEW SUITS (1945). *Novel*

LETTER TO A RETURNING SERVICEMAN (1945). *Essay*

THE SECRET DREAM (1946). *Essay*

RUSSIAN JOURNEY (1946). *Travel*

BRIGHT DAY (1946). *Novel*

THE ARTS UNDER SOCIALISM (1947). *Lecture*

MUSIC AT NIGHT (1947). *Drama*

THEATRE OUTLOOK (1947). *Criticism*

AN INSPECTOR CALLS (1947). *Drama*

JENNY VILLIERS (1947). *Drama*

THE ROSE AND CROWN (1947). *Drama*

THE LINDEN TREE (1948). *Drama*

THE HIGH TOBY (1948). *Drama*
—for the Toy Theatre.

THE GOLDEN FLEECE (1948). *Drama*

DELIGHTS (1949). *Essays*

THE OLYMPIANS (1949). *Opera Libretto*

HOME IS TOMORROW (1949). *Drama*

EVER SINCE PARADISE (1950). *Drama*

GOING UP (1950). *Stories and Sketches*

SUMMER DAY'S DREAM (1950). *Drama*

BRIGHT SHADOW (1950). *Drama*

FESTIVAL AT FARBRIDGE (1951). *Novel*

DRAGON'S MOUTH (1952). *Dramatic Quartet*
—with Jacquetta Hawkes.

PRIVATE ROOMS (1953). *One-Act Play*

TREASURE ON PELICAN (1953). *Drama*

TRY IT AGAIN (1953). *One-Act Play*

MOTHER'S DAY (1953). *Drama*

THE OTHER PLACE (1953). *Stories*

THE MAGICIANS (1954). *Novel*

A GLASS OF BITTER (1954). *One-Act Play*

LOW NOTES ON A HIGH LEVEL (1954). *Fiction*

MR. KETTLE AND MRS. MOON (1955). *Drama*

JOURNEY DOWN A RAINBOW (1955). *Travel*
—with Jacquetta Hawkes.

THE GLASS CAGE (1957). *Drama*

THOUGHTS IN THE WILDERNESS (1957). *Essay*

THE ART OF THE DRAMATIST (1957). *Essay*

TOPSIDE, OR THE FUTURE OF ENGLAND (1958). *Essay*

LITERATURE AND WESTERN MAN (1960). *Criticism*

WILLIAM HAZLITT (1960). *Essay*

SATURN OVER THE WATER (1961). *Novel*

CHARLES DICKENS: A PICTORIAL BIOGRAPHY (1961). *Biography*

THE THIRTY-FIRST OF JUNE (1961). *Novel*

THE SHAPES OF SLEEP (1962). *Novel*

MARGIN RELEASED (1962). *Literary reminiscences*

A SEVERED HEAD (1963). *Drama*
—with Iris Murdoch.

MAN AND TIME (1964). *Essay*

SIR MICHAEL AND SIR GEORGE (1964). *Novel*

WRITERS AND THEIR WORK

General Editor: GEOFFREY BULLOUGH

The first 55 issues in the Series appeared under the General Editorship of T. O. BEACHCROFT
Issues 56–169 appeared under the General Editorship of BONAMY DOBRÉE

General Surveys:

THE DETECTIVE STORY IN BRITAIN:
Julian Symons
THE ENGLISH BIBLE: Donald Coggan
ENGLISH HYMNS: Arthur Pollard
ENGLISH MARITIME WRITING:
Hakluyt to Cook: Oliver Warner
THE ENGLISH SHORT STORY I: & II:
T. O. Beachcroft
ENGLISH SERMONS: Arthur Pollard
ENGLISH TRAVELLERS IN THE
NEAR EAST: Robin Fedden

Sixteenth Century and Earlier:

FRANCIS BACON: J. Max Patrick
CHAUCER: Nevill Coghill
MALORY: M. C. Bradbrook
MARLOWE: Philip Henderson
SIDNEY: Kenneth Muir
SKELTON: Peter Green
SPENSER: Rosemary Freeman
WYATT: Sergio Baldi

Seventeenth Century:

SIR THOMAS BROWNE: Peter Green
BUNYAN: Henri Talon
CAVALIER POETS: Robin Skelton
CONGREVE: Bonamy Dobrée
DONNE: F. Kermode
DRYDEN: Bonamy Dobrée
ENGLISH DIARISTS: Evelyn and
Pepys: M. Willy
JOHN FORD: Clifford Leech
GEORGE HERBERT: T. S. Eliot
HERRICK: John Press
HOBBES: T. E. Jessop
BEN JONSON: J. B. Bamborough
LOCKE: Maurice Cranston
ANDREW MARVELL: John Press
MILTON: E. M. W. Tillyard
SHAKESPEARE: C. J. Sisson
SHAKESPEARE:
CHRONICLES: Clifford Leech
EARLY COMEDIES: Derek Traversi
FINAL PLAYS: F. Kermode
GREAT TRAGEDIES: Kenneth Muir
HISTORIES: L. C. Knights

LATER COMEDIES: G. K. Hunter
POEMS: F. T. Prince
PROBLEM PLAYS: Peter Ure
ROMAN PLAYS: T. J. B. Spencer
THREE METAPHYSICAL POETS:
Margaret Willy
IZAAK WALTON: Margaret Bottrall

Eighteenth Century:

BERKELEY: T. E. Jessop
BLAKE: Kathleen Raine
BOSWELL: P. A. W. Collins
BURKE: T. E. Utley
BURNS: David Daiches
WILLIAM COLLINS: Oswald Doughty
COWPER: N. Nicholson
CRABBE: R. L. Brett
DEFOE: J. R. Sutherland
FIELDING: John Butt
GAY: Oliver Warner
GIBBON: C. V. Wedgwood
GOLDSMITH: A. Norman Jeffares
GRAY: R. W. Ketton-Cremer
JOHNSON: S. C. Roberts
POPE: Ian Jack
RICHARDSON: R. F. Brissenden
SHERIDAN: W. A. Darlington
CHRISTOPHER SMART: G. Grigson
SMOLLETT: Laurence Brander
STEELE AND ADDISON:
A. R. Humphreys
STERNE: D. W. Jefferson
SWIFT: J. Middleton Murry
HORACE WALPOLE: Hugh Honour

Nineteenth Century:

MATTHEW ARNOLD: Kenneth Allott
JANE AUSTEN: S. Townsend Warner
BAGEHOT: N. St. John-Stevas
THE BRONTË SISTERS: P. Bentley
BROWNING: John Bryson
SAMUEL BUTLER: G. D. H. Cole
BYRON: Herbert Read
CARLYLE: David Gascoyne
LEWIS CARROLL: Derek Hudson
CLOUGH: I. Armstrong
COLERIDGE: Kathleen Raine

DE QUINCEY: Hugh Sykes Davies
DICKENS: K. J. Fielding
DISRAELI: Paul Bloomfield
GEORGE ELIOT: Lettice Cooper
FITZGERALD: Joanna Richardson
MRS. GASKELL: Miriam Allott
GISSING: A. C. Ward
THOMAS HARDY: R. A. Scott-James
HAZLITT: J. B. Priestley
HOOD: Laurence Brander
G. M. HOPKINS: Geoffrey Grigson
T. H. HUXLEY: William Irvine
KEATS: Edmund Blunden
LAMB: Edmund Blunden
LANDOR: G. Rostrevor Hamilton
MACAULAY: G. R. Potter
MEREDITH: Phyllis Bartlett
JOHN STUART MILL: M. Cranston
WILLIAM MORRIS: P. Henderson
NEWMAN: J. M. Cameron
PATER: Iain Fletcher
PEACOCK: J. I. M. Stewart
ROSSETTI: Oswald Doughty
RUSKIN: Peter Quennell
SIR WALTER SCOTT: Ian Jack
SHELLEY: Stephen Spender
R. L. STEVENSON: G. B. Stern
SWINBURNE: H. J. C. Grierson
TENNYSON: F. L. Lucas
THACKERAY: Laurence Brander
FRANCIS THOMPSON: P. Butter
TROLLOPE: Hugh Sykes Davies
OSCAR WILDE: James Laver
WORDSWORTH: Helen Darbishire

Twentieth Century:

W. H. AUDEN: Richard Hoggart
HILAIRE BELLOC: Renée Haynes
ARNOLD BENNETT: F. Swinnerton
EDMUND BLUNDEN: Alec M. Hardie
ELIZABETH BOWEN: Jocelyn Brooke
ROBERT BRIDGES: J. Sparrow
ROY CAMPBELL: David Wright
JOYCE CARY: Walter Allen
G. K. CHESTERTON: C. Hollis
WINSTON CHURCHILL: John Connell
R.G. COLLINGWOOD: E.W.F. Tomlin
I. COMPTON-BURNETT:
                    Pamela Hansford Johnson
JOSEPH CONRAD: Oliver Warner

WALTER DE LA MARE: K. Hopkins
NORMAN DOUGLAS: Ian Greenlees
T. S. ELIOT: M. C. Bradbrook
FIRBANK & BETJEMAN: J. Brooke
FORD MADOX FORD: Kenneth Young
E. M. FORSTER: Rex Warner
CHRISTOPHER FRY: Derek Stanford
JOHN GALSWORTHY: R. H. Mottram
ROBERT GRAVES: M. Seymour-Smith
GRAHAM GREENE: Francis Wyndham
L. P. HARTLEY & ANTHONY POWELL:
                    P. Bloomfield and B. Bergonzi
A. E. HOUSMAN: Ian Scott-Kilvert
ALDOUS HUXLEY: Jocelyn Brooke
HENRY JAMES: Michael Swan
JAMES JOYCE: J. I. M. Stewart
RUDYARD KIPLING: B. Dobrée
D. H. LAWRENCE: Kenneth Young
C. DAY LEWIS: Clifford Dyment
WYNDHAM LEWIS: E. W. F. Tomlin
KATHERINE MANSFIELD: Ian Gordon
JOHN MASEFIELD: L. A. G. Strong
SOMERSET MAUGHAM: J. Brophy
EDWIN MUIR: J. C. Hall
J. MIDDLETON MURRY: Philip Mairet
GEORGE ORWELL: Tom Hopkinson
POETS OF 1939-45 WAR:
                    R. N. Currey
POWYS BROTHERS: R. C. Churchill
J. B. PRIESTLEY: Ivor Brown
HERBERT READ: Francis Berry
BERTRAND RUSSELL: Alan Dorward
BERNARD SHAW: A. C. Ward
EDITH SITWELL: John Lehmann
OSBERT SITWELL: Roger Fulford
C. P. SNOW: William Cooper
STRACHEY: R. A. Scott-James
SYNGE & LADY GREGORY:
                    E. Coxhead
DYLAN THOMAS: G. S. Fraser
EDWARD THOMAS: Vernon Scannell
G. M. TREVELYAN: J. H. Plumb
WAR POETS: 1914-18: E. Blunden
EVELYN WAUGH: Christopher Hollis
H. G. WELLS: Montgomery Belgion
CHARLES WILLIAMS: J. Heath-Stubbs
VIRGINIA WOOLF: Bernard Blackstone
W. B. YEATS: G. S. Fraser
ANDREW YOUNG & R. S. THOMAS:
                    L. Clark and R. G. Thomas